Timeline of Ancient Egypt

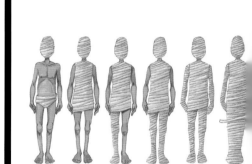

1186–1089 B.C.
Royal tombs in the Valley of the Kings plundered for treasure by robbers.

c.2686 B.C.
Step pyramid at Saqqara built by Djoser.

c.3200 B.C.
Hieroglyphics developed.

c.1700 B.C.
Earliest evidence of diagnostic medicine in Egypt.

c.5000 B.C.
People settle along the Nile Delta.

2135–1986 B.C.
Egypt split into two regions, ruled from Herakleopolis in the north and Thebes in the south.

1069–1043 B.C.
Noticeable advancement in mummification techniques.

A.D. 395
Egyptian hieroglyphics no longer used or understood.

2890–2686 B.C.
Wooden coffins used and corpses wrapped in resin-soaked bandages.

1333–1324 B.C.
Reign of Tutankhamen.

c.A.D. 1000

ractice of "eating
nummy" begins.

1922

Archeologist Howard Carter
discovers the tomb of King
Tutankhamen.

1834

First public mummy
unwrapping performed by
Dr. Thomas J. Pettigrew.

1822

Jean-François
Champollion decodes
ieroglyphics using the
Rosetta Stone,
discovered in 1799.

1996

Zahi Hawass discovers
the Valley of the
Golden Mummies.

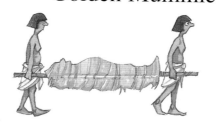

2005

Scientists create a
bust of King
Tutankhamen based
on 3-D CT scans of
his 3,300-year-old
mummy.

1880

Flinders Petrie arrives in Egypt to begin
the serious study of Egyptology.

Map of Ancient Egypt

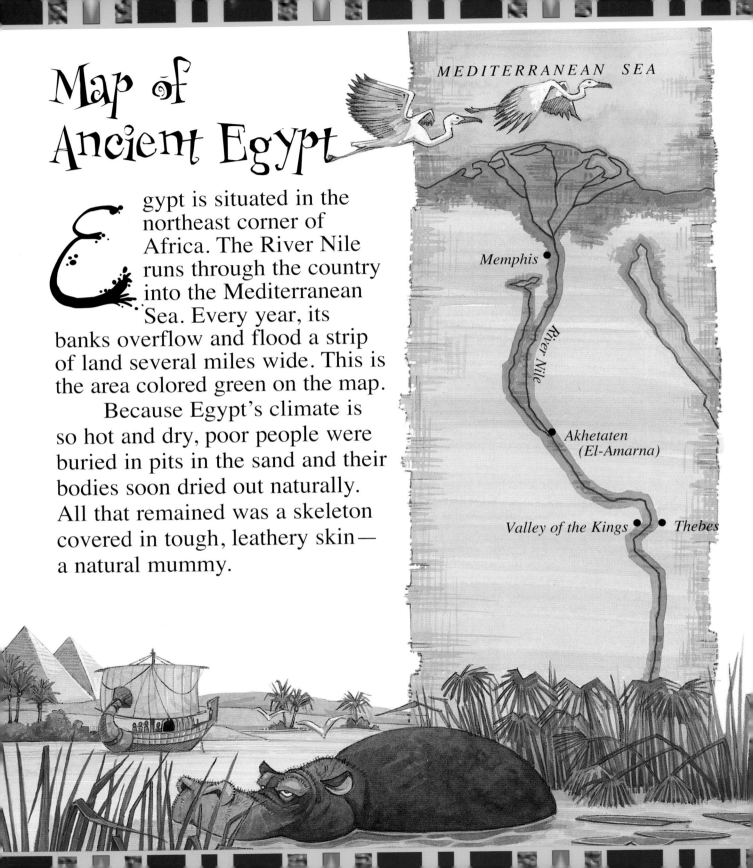

MEDITERRANEAN SEA

Egypt is situated in the northeast corner of Africa. The River Nile runs through the country into the Mediterranean Sea. Every year, its banks overflow and flood a strip of land several miles wide. This is the area colored green on the map.

Because Egypt's climate is so hot and dry, poor people were buried in pits in the sand and their bodies soon dried out naturally. All that remained was a skeleton covered in tough, leathery skin— a natural mummy.

Memphis

River Nile

Akhetaten
(El-Amarna)

Valley of the Kings

Thebes

Author:
David Stewart has written many non-fiction books for children. He lives in Brighton with his wife and young son.

Artist:
David Antram was born in Brighton, England, in 1958. He studied at Eastbourne College of Art and then worked in advertising for 15 years before becoming a full-time artist. He has illustrated many children's non-fiction books.

Series Creator:
David Salariya was born in Dundee, Scotland. He has illustrated a wide range of books and has created and designed many new series for publishers both in the U.K. and overseas. In 1989 he established the Salariya Book Company. He lives in Brighton with his wife, the illustrator Shirley Willis, and their son.

Editor:
Karen Barker Smith

Editorial Assistant:
Stephanie Cole

© The Salariya Book Company Ltd MMXIII

Published in Great Britain in 2013 by
The Salariya Book Company Ltd
25 Marlborough Place, Brighton BN1 1UB

ISBN-13: 978-0-531-27501-6 (lib. bdg.)   978-0-531-28026-3 (pbk.)

Published in 2013 in the United States
by Franklin Watts
An imprint of Scholastic Inc.
Published simultaneously in Canada.

A CIP catalog record for this book is available
from the Library of Congress.

Printed and bound in Shanghai, China.
Printed on paper from sustainable sources.
Reprinted in 2014.
3 4 5 6 7 8 9 10 R 21 20 19 18 17 16 15 14

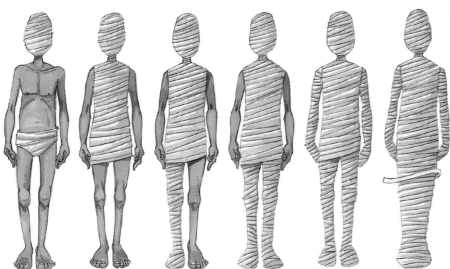

You Wouldn't Want to Be an Egyptian Mummy!

Disgusting Things You'd Rather Not Know

Written by
David Stewart

Illustrated by
David Antram

Created and designed by
David Salariya

W
FRANKLIN WATTS
A Division of Grolier Publishing
NEW YORK • LONDON • HONG KONG • SYDNEY
DANBURY, CONNECTICUT

Contents

Introduction

Ancient Egypt as we know it began about 5,000 years ago beside the River Nile in northern Africa. The Nile floods made this land very fertile, although beyond it lay a vast area of blistering desert thought to be inhabited by demons.

Ancient Egyptian history spans thirty centuries, and throughout this time the country was ruled by kings called pharaohs. The people believed that the pharaoh was a living god, and so it was very important to keep him happy. The pharaohs had huge monuments built for them so that they would always be remembered. Ancient Egyptians believed in an afterlife and thought that by saying the name of a dead person, you could make them live forever. Another way to achieve immortality was to preserve the body of a person once they had died, and wrap them up in linen bandages. This process is called mummification.

Now cast yourself back 3,000 years. You are a wealthy ancient Egyptian on the point of death, and you want to make yourself immortal. To achieve this, you

will have to go through the expensive and complicated process of becoming a mummy. Get ready, as you are about to...drop dead.

Dead? Off to the Embalmers!

What You Will Need:

YOUR DEAD BODY. When you die, the embalmers will take your body away as soon as possible.

First it will be taken to a "tent of purification," called an *ibu*.

LINEN. Like most ancient Egyptians, you will have saved linen throughout your life to use as mummification bandages.

OILS. Perfumes and oils will make your skin smooth and sweet-smelling.

A PRIEST. You will need a priest to act as chief embalmer. He should wear a mask of Anubis, god of embalming (right).

Ancient Egyptians take a lot of trouble preparing for the afterlife. They believe that every person has three spirits that survive after death, but only if the body is preserved. These are the *ka*, the person's life force; the *ba*, the spirit of the person's personality; and the *akh*, the glorified soul.

The dead body is preserved by the complicated processes of embalming and mummification. Everyone who can afford it makes elaborate preparations for this.

What Can You Afford?

CHEAP. The body is injected with cedar oil, which makes its insides liquefy and drain out. It is then dried out in a natural salt called natron.

MID-RANGE. The organs are removed and embalmed. The body is dried out in natron and then completely wrapped up in strips of linen.

LUXURY. The same as mid-range, but with a portrait mask. This is made of cartonnage (a mixture of plaster linen, and resin), or even solid gold

The men who practice the art of embalming are highly respected, as they are responsible for preparing you for eternal life.

Handy Hint

Your body should be labeled with a wooden tag to avoid any mix-ups later.

I'm sure he was taller...

The body is washed with a solution of natron dissolved in water.

Covering a dead body in natron salt makes it shriveled and shrunken.

Removing the Organs
What You Will Need:

YOUR FRESHLY SCRUBBED BODY along with all necessary priests and assistants.

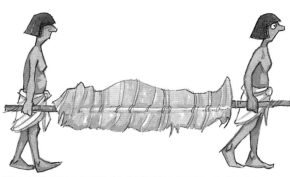

TOOLS. Various tools and surgical instruments will be needed to clean out your body and remove certain organs.

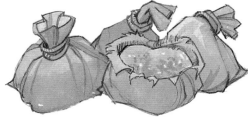

NATRON SALT. This will be used to dry out your body once the organs have been removed.

KNIFE. The "slicer" will use a ceremonial flint knife to cut your body open.

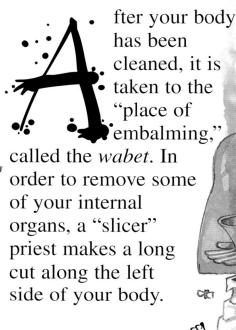

After your body has been cleaned, it is taken to the "place of embalming," called the *wabet*. In order to remove some of your internal organs, a "slicer" priest makes a long cut along the left side of your body.

Sniff!

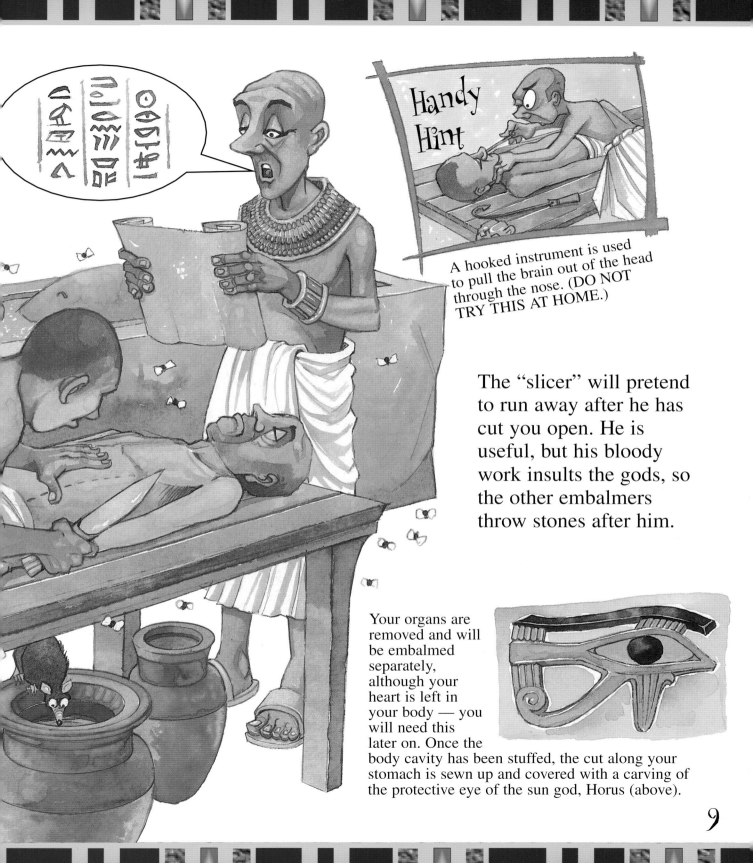

A hooked instrument is used to pull the brain out of the head through the nose. (DO NOT TRY THIS AT HOME.)

The "slicer" will pretend to run away after he has cut you open. He is useful, but his bloody work insults the gods, so the other embalmers throw stones after him.

Your organs are removed and will be embalmed separately, although your heart is left in your body — you will need this later on. Once the body cavity has been stuffed, the cut along your stomach is sewn up and covered with a carving of the protective eye of the sun god, Horus (above).

9

Storing the Organs

What You Will Need:

YOUR LIVER will be stored in a jar with the human head of the god Imsety on it.

YOUR LUNGS are stored in the jar protected by the god Hapy, who has the head of a baboon.

YOUR STOMACH is placed in the jar with the jackal head of the god Duamutef on it.

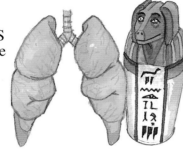

YOUR INTESTINES are kept in the jar that has on it the falcon head of the god Qebehsenuef.

Your liver, lungs, stomach, and intestines are removed through the incision in your side. Once the organs have been completely removed, they are stored in canopic jars. Each jar is protected by one of the four sons of the god Horus, and the lid of each jar is in the shape of its protector god's head.

Your body is washed out with palm wine and will now be soaked in natron for forty days to dry it out.

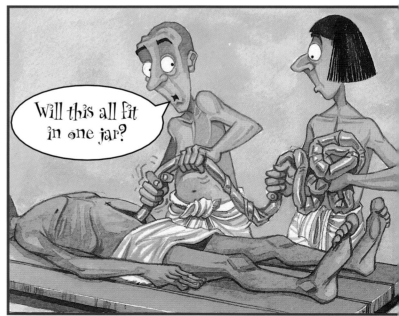

Will this all fit in one jar?

A Step-By-Step Guide to Embalming:

INTESTINES are a problem, as they can be very long. Once removed, soak in natron. Turn occasionally.

10

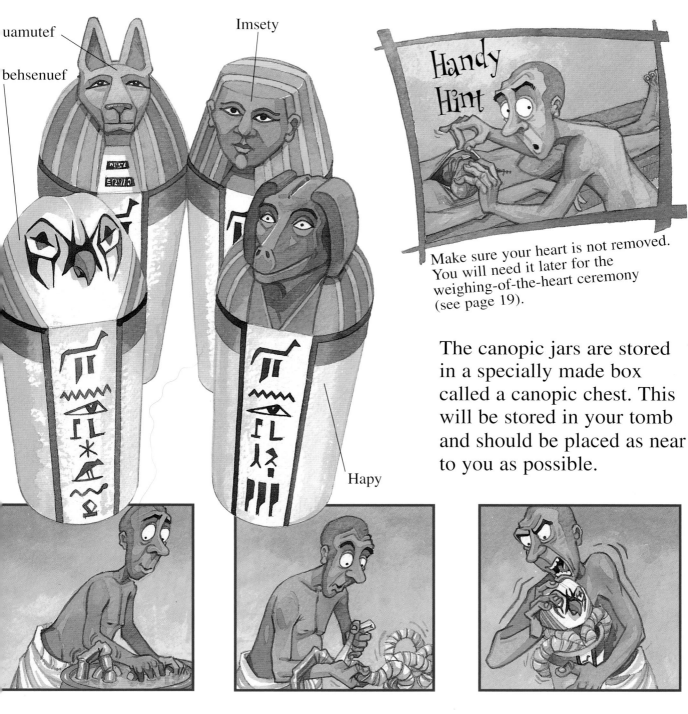

uamutef

behsenuef

Imsety

Hapy

Handy Hint

Make sure your heart is not removed. You will need it later for the weighing-of-the-heart ceremony (see page 19).

The canopic jars are stored in a specially made box called a canopic chest. This will be stored in your tomb and should be placed as near to you as possible.

AFTER FORTY DAYS, remove from the natron and check that there is no moisture left in them.

IF THE INTESTINES are completely dried, they are ready to be wrapped in linen.

THE ORGAN can now be placed in its canopic jar. Ideally, the lid should fit tightly.

11

Get Stuffed!

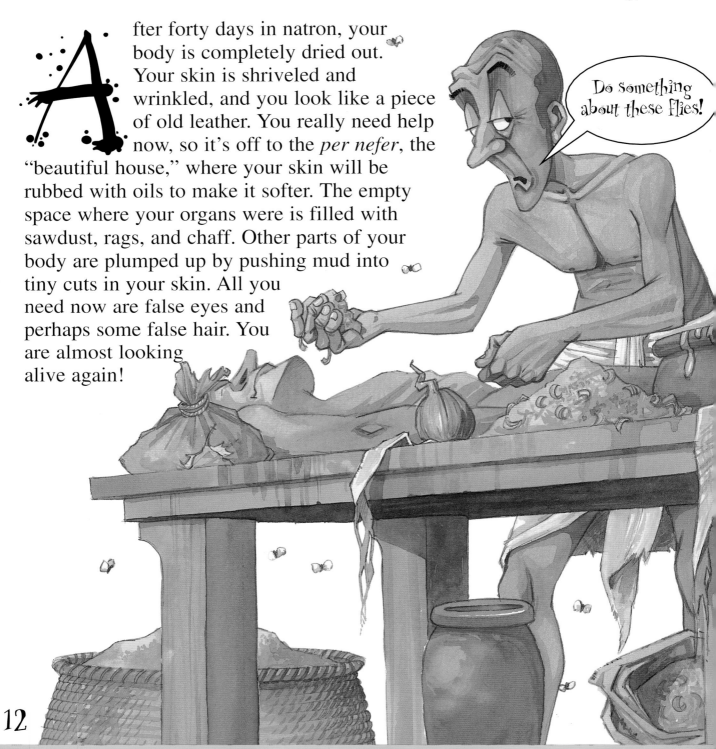

After forty days in natron, your body is completely dried out. Your skin is shriveled and wrinkled, and you look like a piece of old leather. You really need help now, so it's off to the *per nefer*, the "beautiful house," where your skin will be rubbed with oils to make it softer. The empty space where your organs were is filled with sawdust, rags, and chaff. Other parts of your body are plumped up by pushing mud into tiny cuts in your skin. All you need now are false eyes and perhaps some false hair. You are almost looking alive again!

Do something about these flies!

False eyes can be made out of onions. As they have strong antiseptic qualities, they can also be stuffed into the body cavity.

Eye eye, boss!

Handy Hint

What You Will Need:

PALM WINE and juniper oil are used to sterilize the body.

FRANKINCENSE, a highly valued fragrant gum resin, makes the body smell sweet.

SAWDUST, chaff, sand, and rags are used to stuff the body cavity.

MOLTEN RESIN is used to cover the whole body once it has been stuffed.

13

Bound for the Tomb
What You Will Need:

The scarab amulet (above) has a special purpose (see page 19)

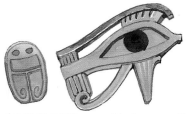

AMULETS, small charms that will provide you with magical protection, should be tucked in your bandages.

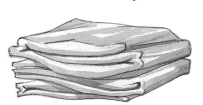

LINEN WRAPPINGS are essential, as wool is thought to be unclean.

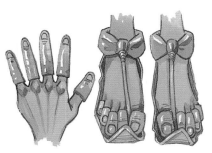

FINGER AND TOE STALLS are only used in luxury mummifications. Can you afford these?

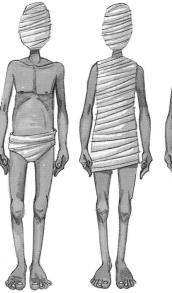

A PORTRAIT MASK might be placed over your head once you are wrapped.

The embalmer's work is almost done, and soon you will be a mummy. All you need now are your wrappings. It will take 15 days to wrap you up, and you will need 20 layers of linen bandages. If you are sensible, you will have been saving linen your whole life. Egyptian temples are full of statues that are dressed in new linen every day, so you could have bought plenty of second-hand linen there.

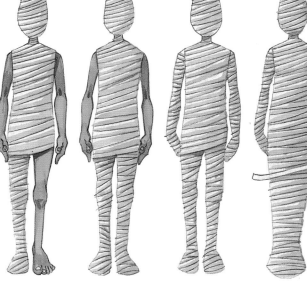

Wrapping the Mummy

Different bandagers work in different ways — some prefer to start with the head and work their way down the body (above). Resin is used to glue the bandages together.

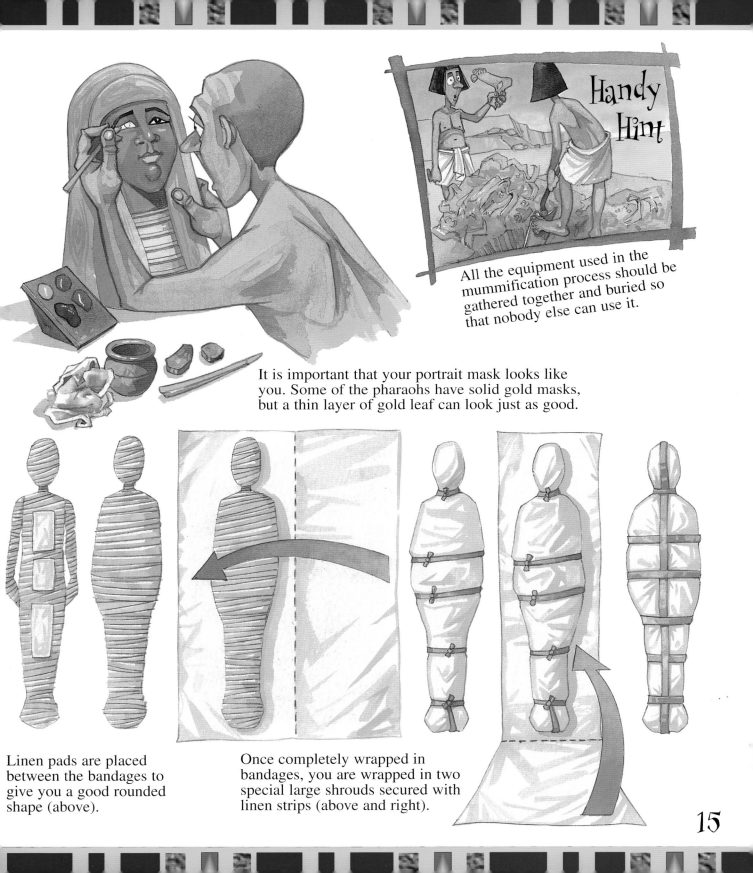

All the equipment used in the mummification process should be gathered together and buried so that nobody else can use it.

It is important that your portrait mask looks like you. Some of the pharaohs have solid gold masks, but a thin layer of gold leaf can look just as good.

Linen pads are placed between the bandages to give you a good rounded shape (above).

Once completely wrapped in bandages, you are wrapped in two special large shrouds secured with linen strips (above and right).

15

The Coffins
What You Will Need:

SKILLED CARPENTERS are always in demand in ancient Egypt. Make sure yours works to a high standard and finishes on time.

WOOD is very valuable since most of it has to be imported. The best wood, if you can afford it, is cedar from Lebanon.

Adze

Wooden mallets

Saw

Chisel

Bowdrill

CARPENTER'S TOOLS are made of wood or stone, and some have blades made of bronze.

PAINTS are made by grinding up semi-precious stones and mixing the powder with plant gum.

Paint

Palette

Brush

Once you have been wrapped, you will need a good wooden coffin. If you are very wealthy, you could have as many as three coffins all fitting snugly inside one another. Make sure that they have pictures of the gods and all the correct spells painted on them to protect you. Of course, they should also have plenty of hieroglyphs singing your praises written on them. This nest of coffins will finally be placed in your tomb inside a large stone coffin called a sarcophagus.

Weepers and Wailers

What You Will Need:

MOURNERS should be hired professionals. They should sob and wail loudly, wearing blue dresses (the color of mourning) and throwing ash on themselves.

PRIESTS burn sweet smelling incense, recite prayers, and perform the opening-of-the-mouth ceremony.

SACRED TOOLS are needed for the opening of the mouth ceremony, which will restore the body's spirit to it.

YOUR TOMB will be both a burial place and a place for your family to leave food for you and to commune with your *ba*.

You have now been dead for seventy days, and today is the day of your funeral. You are finally about to enter the afterlife! You will be buried on the western side of the river, where the sun sets. Your coffin is taken there by boat and is then placed on a sledge and pulled to your tomb. A priest leads a procession of mourners, followed by bearers carrying food offerings and all the objects you will need in the afterlife.

Opening-of-the-Mouth Ceremony

This takes place in front of your tomb. A priest touches your "lips" with symbolic tools to restore your senses and allow your departed soul to return.

Handy Hint

The scarab beetle amulet prevents your guilty secrets from being found out at the weighing-of-the-heart ceremony.

The Weighing of the Heart

Your spirit is led to a scale by Anubis, who weighs your heart against the feather of truth. The result is recorded by the ibis-headed god, Thoth. A monster, Ammut, waits to eat the heart if it has been made too heavy by its bad deeds.

What was his name again?

Anubis

Thoth

Ammut

Feather

Heart

What a Mummy Needs
(Really, Really Needs) for a Blissful Afterlife

Have the walls of your tomb painted with pictures of you wearing your best clothes in the kind of afterlife you want to enjoy. Your tomb should be stocked with the things you needed when you were alive: food, clothes, furniture, weapons, and tools.

THE BOOK OF THE DEAD is a guidebook of spells to help you through the horrors of the underworld.

YOUR *BA*, the spirit of your personality, is able to leave your tomb during the day, but will always return at night.

YOUR *KA*, or spirit double, will remain with you in your tomb at all times.

TOMB OFFERINGS. It is the duty of your relatives to visit your tomb with gifts of food so that you don't go hungry. As long as people remember you and speak your name, you will enjoy everlasting life.

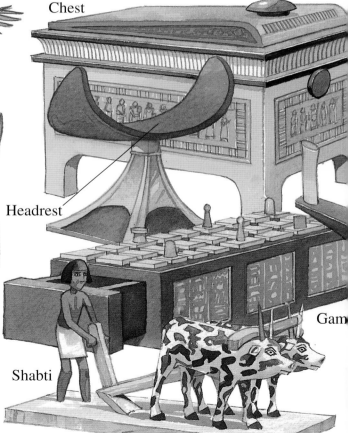

Chest

Headrest

Shabti

Gam

Finding good servants in the next world might be difficult, so take plenty of *shabtis* to do your work for you.

Once your tomb has been sealed, your soul has battled its way through the underworld, and your heart has been weighed against the feather of truth, you can at last begin to enjoy your afterlife! Now nothing can disturb you...or can it?

Wig box

Stool

Wine

Food

Grapes

Boat

Bread

Figs

Shabtis

21

Tomb Robbers

What They Want:

LINEN is very valuable because of the time it can take to weave even the smallest amount.

GLASS is scarce in ancient Egypt. Since it can be melted down and made into new objects, stolen glass cannot be traced.

GOLD JEWELRY. The jewels can be pried out and the gold melted down and re-used.

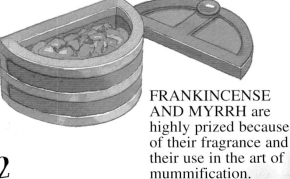

FRANKINCENSE AND MYRRH are highly prized because of their fragrance and their use in the art of mummification.

Once your tomb doors are firmly closed and sealed, you may think you are ready for eternal rest. No such luck! Even before the mourners at your funeral have had time to go home, unwanted visitors are on their way — tomb robbers have started tunneling toward you. If they steal even one small piece of jewelry from you, it could make them very rich, so they feel it's worth taking the risk of torture and death if they are caught. Mummies ripped open by robbers looking for treasure have to be re-wrapped, sometimes gaining extra heads or legs in the process!

It's mine, all mine!

Animal Mummies

Four Varieties of Animal Mummies:

FOOD. A cut of meat can be embalmed and put in a special box for you to enjoy in the afterlife.

PETS. Your pet can be mummified at the same time as you, whether it is ready to join the afterlife or not.

CULT ANIMALS. Some animals, like this Ibis bull, are mummified, as they are believed to have special powers and are treated like gods.

VOTIVE OFFERING. A gift of a specially embalmed animal can be given to please a god.

Ancient Egyptians worry that mummies might get hungry in the afterlife, so they leave a piece of meat in the tomb. An animal's leg can be embalmed for use as mummy food. Mummified Ibis bulls are worshiped at sacred sites and are thought to be messengers to the gods. Before you died, you might have made a special journey to a temple to buy an embalmed animal as a gift for a god.

Beware of forgeries. Traders sometimes make animal mummies out of sticks and feathers.

I think I'll take a cat instead.

Ancient Egyptians fear that the afterlife might get lonely. Unfortunate pets, like this dog and cat, may be killed and embalmed to keep you company.

25

Eternal Rest?
Some Odd Uses for Mummies:

PAINT. A horrified artist, who found that the paint he was using was made from ground-up human mummy remains, gave the tubes of paint a decent burial.

PAPER. An outbreak of cholera was allegedly caused when butchers used brown paper made from linen mummy wrappings to wrap their meat.

FERTILIZER. Mummified cats shipped from Egypt to Europe were used as fertilizer until a public outcry stopped the practice.

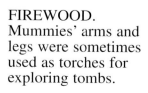

FIREWOOD. Mummies' arms and legs were sometimes used as torches for exploring tombs.

An invitation to a mummy unwrapping

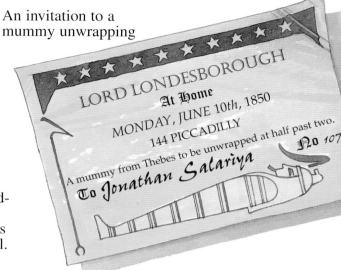

LORD LONDESBOROUGH
At Home
MONDAY, JUNE 10th, 1850
144 PICCADILLY
A mummy from Thebes to be unwrapped at half past two.
No 107
To Jonathan Salariya

Ooohhh!

Gas

By the 19th century A.D., 2,800 years after your death, you may think you have found eternal peace at last. Wrong! It becomes fashionable among the wealthy to travel to Egypt and buy mummies as souvenirs of their travels. Unfortunately for you, it also becomes fashionable to publicly unwrap mummies. No one is interested in you, however — only the magic amulets tucked in your wrappings. If you are lucky, you may be re-wrapped and put in a museum.

Handy Hint

Ground-up mummies are used as an ointment for skin complaints, mixed with butter and rubbed onto the skin.

This amulet was to keep the secrets of the heart....

Uurghh!

Whiff! Whiff!

Strange Afterlives
Well-Traveled Mummies:

BY PLANE. The mummy of the great pharaoh Ramesses II was flown to Paris for treatment of a fungal growth. The 3,300-year-old mummy had "monarch (deceased)" stamped on his passport. The treatment was a success.

MUMMY OVERBOARD! Tourists who had bought a mummy as a souvenir changed their minds about taking it home because of its terrible smell. They threw it in the River Nile.

FAR FROM HOME. A mummy purchased by a tourist in Aswan was later identified as the body of an English engineer who had recently died there.

Some mummies have become celebrities in more recent years. Horror stories about mummies coming back to life were popular in the 19th century and helped to create the legends associated with Tutankhamun, the most famous mummy in the world. His largely untouched tomb, full of treasures, was discovered by the archaeologist Howard Carter in 1922. His sponsor was Lord Carnarvon, who died from an infected mosquito bite soon after the tomb was opened. His death gave rise to the myth of the "pharaoh's curse," which would bring death to anyone who entered the tomb.

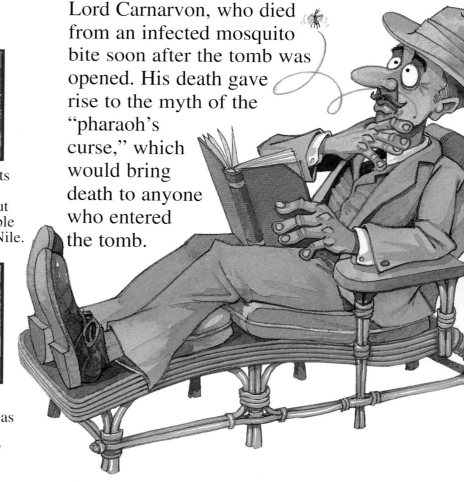

Famous Mummies

A lot of oil!

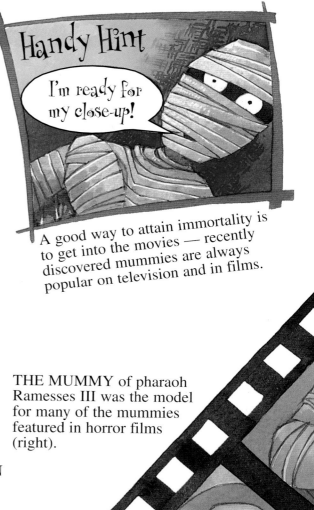

Handy Hint

I'm ready for my close-up!

A good way to attain immortality is to get into the movies — recently discovered mummies are always popular on television and in films.

KING TUTANKHAMUN'S mummy suffered badly from the amount of oils used in the mummification process. His flesh stuck to the inside of his coffin, meaning that his mummy had to be cut up to remove it. His ribs are still missing.

THE MUMMY of pharaoh Ramesses III was the model for many of the mummies featured in horror films (right).

AN ANCIENT EGYPTIAN MUMMY known as the "screaming mummy" (left) was buried alive and wrapped in sheepskin, probably as a punishment.

Groan!

Glossary

Adze An axelike tool with the blade set in the handle at a right angle.

Akh According to ancient Egyptian belief, the *akh* was one of three spirits released at a person's death and it represented the higher soul.

Ammut A demon of the underworld who attended the weighing-of-the-heart test and ate the heart of anybody who failed it.

Amulet A small object, like a lucky charm, believed to provide magical protection to the person wearing it.

Anubis The jackal-headed god of embalming.

Ba One of the three spirits released when someone died. It represented the person's character, or personality.

Book of the Dead A collection of spells and prayers left in tombs to help the dead in the underworld.

Canopic jars The set of four jars in which the embalmed lungs, stomach,

liver, and intestines were stored.

Cartonnage Material made from pulped linen etc., often used to make the masks for Egyptian mummies.

Chaff Chopped up hay and straw, often used to stuff the body cavities of dead people once their organs had been removed.

Embalming The practice of preserving dead bodies.

Finger and toe stalls Metal sheaths, sometimes made of gold, placed over the ends of an embalmed body's fingers and toes.

Hieroglyphs The ancient Egyptian writing system, which consists of pictures representing sounds.

Horus The son of the gods Isis and Osiris. Horus had the head of a falcon and was the sun god.

Ibu "Tent of purification"; the first place a body was taken after death.

Ka The *ka* was a person's life force. When the person died, his *ka* lived on in his mummy.

Mummy An embalmed body wrapped in linen bandages. The word "mummy" comes from the Persian word *mummiya*, meaning "pitch" or "bitumen". Some Egyptian mummies blackened over time and gave rise to the incorrect belief that bitumen was the embalming agent used.

Natron A form of natural salt used for drying out the body during the mummification process.

Per nefer The place where embalmed bodies were rubbed with perfumed oils, stuffed, and given false eyes and hair. It means "beautiful house."

Sarcophagus A large outer coffin, usually made of stone.

Shabtis Pottery figurines in human shape buried with a mummy. They were called upon to do manual labor for the dead person in the underworld.

Thoth The god of wisdom and writing. Sometimes he is shown as an ibis, sometimes a baboon.

Votive offerings Special gifts for the gods, usually left in temples or other holy places.

Wabet The place where a body is taken to have its organs removed and to be dried out in natron salt. It means the "place of embalming."

Index

Ancient Egyptian Life

Wildlife and Plants

The Egyptian desert is the home of lions, jackals, antelope, gazelle, and ibex. Very little grows in the desert aside from thorn trees. In contrast, the valley is green with growing crops and shade trees. The most common trees are the date palm; the dom palm, which has a nutlike fruit; and the sycamore fig. The Nile water lily is a favorite flower.

Towns and Villages

There are isolated villages in the western hills, built for workers who make the royal tombs, but most people live by the river. Villages are perched on land that the floodwater does not cover. Large cities exist on the east bank but not on the west bank. That is where the dead are buried. The ancient Egyptians believed that the dead traveled westward, like the sun. And, like the sun, they would wake to a new life.

The Pharaoh

The kings of ancient Egypt were given the title of *pharaoh*, which means "great house." The pharaohs were very powerful—the Egyptians believed each one was a living god. The pharaoh used local governors and huge numbers of officials to carry out his orders. People believed that it was the influence of the pharaoh that ensured that the river flooded each year.

Water Is Life

The river gives life, not only to humans but to a multitude of wild creatures. Its waters are full of fish, many of which are edible, like the gray mullet and Nile perch. The papyrus reeds of the delta and other marshy areas teem with bird life— ducks, teal, crane, quail, and ibis. Wildcats stalk prey there; mongooses hunt for eggs. Hippopotamuses wallow in the marshy pools and crocodiles glide silently by.

Taming the Nile

All of the farmers' crops depend on the waters of the Nile. Dikes prevent floodwater from draining away and canals take it to the farmers' fields. If careless landowners let their canals leak, they deprive other people of water. One of the most important departments of the king's government looks after the sharing of water along more than 62 miles (100 kilometers) of river.

Dangers and Death

You might expect that the Egyptians feared crocodiles and diseases, but evil spirits were what they feared most of all. They believed that most misfortunes were caused by evil spirits. Childbirth was dangerous for both mothers and babies, many of whom died. This accounts for the short life expectancy of ancient Egyptians—probably around 36 years. Many people lived much longer. The pharaoh Pepi II ruled for 94 years, the longest reign in history that we know of.

Egyptian Gods

The gods played a large part in the lives of the ancient Egyptians. It was very important to stay in the gods' favor, for without their help, disasters might happen. Egyptians held great festivals in honor of the gods and built them huge temples. The pharaohs liked building these temples; they were monuments the pharaohs could be remembered by.

Did You Know?

- Ancient Egypt was the first civilization to make use of the sciences, including math and medicine.
- Ancient Egyptians were the first to make bread rise by adding yeast.
- Our alphabet is said to have been influenced by Egyptian hieroglyphs, which used 24 symbols for consonants, along with many other symbols.
- Scissors, combs, toothbrushes, and toothpaste, plus the lock and key, the weaving loom, drums, and oil lamps were all invented in ancient Egypt.

Top Creepy Mummies

"Ginger," the First Egyptian Mummy Ginger has been in the British Museum in London for more than 100 years. The high humidity in the museum is causing Ginger's skin to peel off!

Tutankhamen Poor Tutankhamen suffered from a cleft palate, a clubfoot, and various long-term illnesses. He broke his leg shortly before his death—but he probably died of malaria.

Queen Henuttawy The embalmers overdid the stuffing on Queen Henuttawy's cheeks and it burst through her skin.

Animal Mummies Some mummies of sacred bulls contain only the head of the animal. What happened to the rest? Was it eaten by the priests?

Queen Nodjmet Nodjmet's face was badly scarred when tomb robbers cut through her wrappings in search of valuable jewelry.

Ramesses II This pharaoh had a thin neck, and the embalmers accidentally knocked his head off. They reattached the head with a piece of wood.

Nesyamun Nesyamun's mummy, preserved at Leeds Museum in England, was damaged by a bomb during World War II. He was lucky: all other mummies at the museum were completely destroyed.

Seqenenre Tao II The embalmers had to do a rush job on this pharaoh's body, because it had already begun to rot before they started working on it.

The "Screaming Mummy" In 1886, Gaston Maspero unwrapped the body of a young man, whose face was screaming in agony, his hands and feet tightly bound.

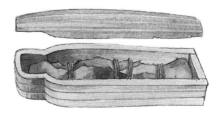